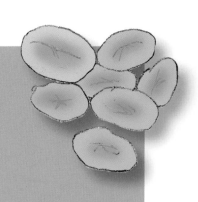

Healthy Eating

Sweets and Snacks

Susan Martineau
and Hel James

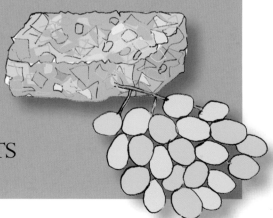

W

FRANKLIN WATTS
LONDON • SYDNEY

An Appleseed Editions book

First published in 2006 by
Franklin Watts
338 Euston Road, London NW1 3BH

Franklin Watts Australia
Hachette Children's Books
Level 17/207 Kent Street
Sydney NSW 2000

Created by Appleseed Editions Ltd,
Well House, Friars Hill, Guestling, East Sussex TN35 4ET

Designed and illustrated by Helen James
Edited by Jinny Johnson

ISBN-10: 0-7496-6723-0
ISBN-13: 978-0-7496-6723-8
Dewey Classification: 641.3

A CIP catalogue for this book is available from the British Library

Photographs: 10-11 Owen Franken/Corbis; 12 Bob Krist/Corbis; 13 Ed Young/Corbis; 16 Envision/Corbis;
18 George D. Lepp/Corbis; 19 M. ou Me. Desjeux, Bernard/Corbis; 20 Richard T. Nowitz;
22 Gary Houlder/Corbis; 24 Pitchal Frederic/Corbis Sygma; 26-27 Ludovic Maisant/Corbis:
Front cover: Ralph A. Clevenger/Corbis

Printed and bound in Thailand

Contents

Food for health

Our bodies are like amazing machines. Just like machines, we need the right sort of fuel to give us energy and to keep us working properly.

If we don't eat the kind of food we need to keep us healthy we may become ill or feel tired and grumpy. Our bodies don't really like it if we eat too much of one sort of food, like cakes or chips.

We need a balanced diet. That means eating different sorts of good food in the right amounts.

You'll be surprised at how much there is to know about where our food comes from and why some kinds of food are better for us than others. Finding out about food is great fun and very tasty!

Can we go to the sweetshop now?

A balanced plateful!

The good things or nutrients our bodies need come from different kinds of food. Let's have a look at what your plate should have on it. It all looks delicious!

Rice, bread and pasta

These foods contain carbohydrates and they give us energy. They are also called starchy foods. About a third of your food should come from this group.

Fruit and vegetables

Rice, bread and pasta

A juicy peach is a great snack.

Fruit and vegetables

These are full of great vitamins and minerals and fibre. They do all kinds of useful jobs in your body to help keep you healthy. About a third of our food should come from this group.

Milk, yogurt and cheese

These dairy foods give us protein and also calcium to make strong bones and teeth.

Meat, fish and eggs

Protein from these helps your body grow and repair itself. They are body-building foods and you need to eat some of them every day.

Sugar and fats

We only need small amounts of these. Too much can be bad for our teeth and make us fat.

Milk, yogurt and cheese

Sugar and fats

Meat, fish and eggs

Water

We need to drink at least 6 glasses of water every day.

Sugar and fat attack!

Sweets are full of sugar. Sugar gives us a quick burst of energy but doesn't have any healthy nutrients. Too much sugar is also bad for your teeth.

Most of the other snacks we eat, like crisps and chips, are full of fat and sometimes they are very salty too. Too much fat and too much salt are not good for our bodies. Biscuits and cakes can be nice to eat, but they are also very fatty. We do need some fat in our balanced diet but not too much!

Shall I buy a bag of sweets today?

Try and think about the balanced plateful when you are choosing a snack. Swap your crisps for some plain popcorn or grab a piece of juicy fruit instead of a bag of sweets.

Everyone likes to eat sweets sometimes, but it's best for your body to choose healthier snacks.

Sweet stuff

It is hard to say 'no thanks' when your friends offer you a sweet. There are so many different sorts of sweets in the shops to tempt us, but they are all made with loads of sugar. We need to be careful not to eat too many of them.

Your teeth don't like it when you eat too many sweets. Hard sweets, like lollipops, take ages to finish and it is like giving your teeth a bath in sugar. This gives bacteria a chance to make something called acid that attacks your teeth!

Dried apricots

Have some fresh or dried fruit instead of sweets. It is full of vitamins and minerals. Dried apricots and raisins give your body iron that is good for your blood.

Raisins are dried grapes.

Grapes are a great snack too.

Look after your teeth by cleaning them twice day.

11

Chocolate

Chocolate is made from cocoa beans. These beans are the seeds of the cacao tree that grows in South America, Africa and Indonesia. The cocoa beans grow inside large pods on the tree.

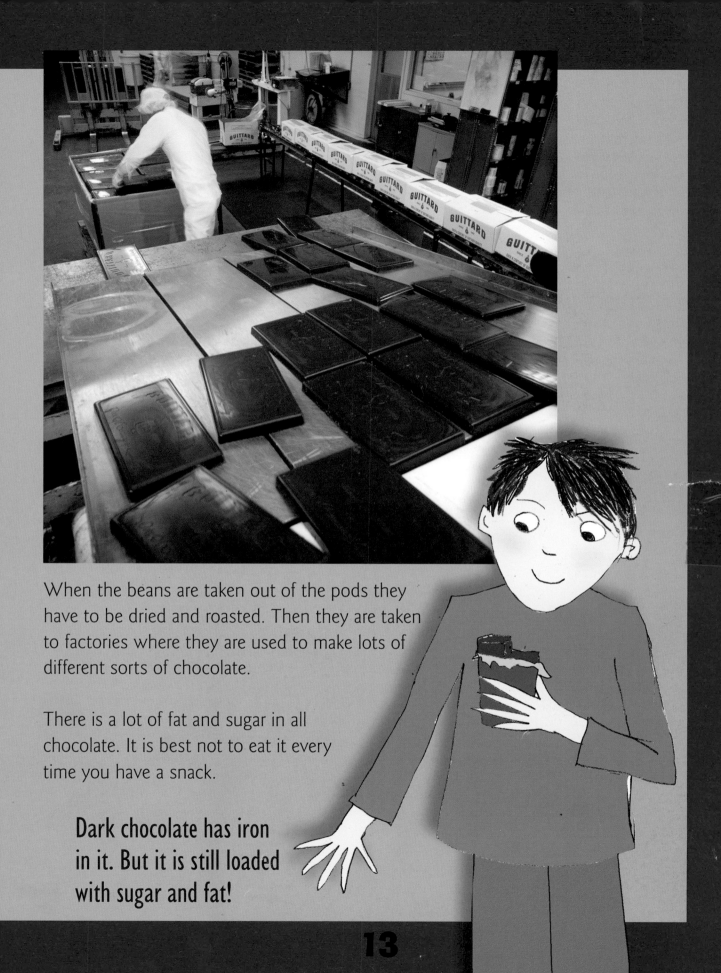

When the beans are taken out of the pods they have to be dried and roasted. Then they are taken to factories where they are used to make lots of different sorts of chocolate.

There is a lot of fat and sugar in all chocolate. It is best not to eat it every time you have a snack.

Dark chocolate has iron in it. But it is still loaded with sugar and fat!

Cakes, buns and biscuits

Eating a cake or munching some biscuits for your snack is all right from time to time, but all cakes, buns and biscuits contain a lot of fat and sugar. Have a look at the labels on their packets the next time you are in a food shop to spot the sugar and fat.

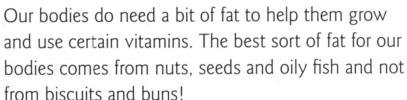

Our bodies do need a bit of fat to help them grow and use certain vitamins. The best sort of fat for our bodies comes from nuts, seeds and oily fish and not from biscuits and buns!

When you get home from school, snack on some breakfast cereal or a pile of breadsticks dunked in your favourite dip.

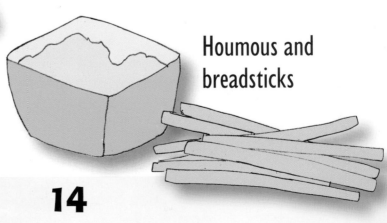

Houmous and breadsticks

Eat some fresh fruit like a banana or a bunch of grapes instead of a biscuit. Your body will love all the vitamins in them.

If you want cakes or biscuits sometimes, try making your own. That way you know exactly how much fat and sugar is in them.

Make flapjacks with healthy oats.

Make muffins with wholemeal flour.

Ice cream
and lollies

Ice cream is made from milk, cream and sugar. It can be made at home, but most of us eat ice cream that has been made in factories. All kinds of flavourings and colours are added to the ice cream.

The mixture is stirred in huge vats as it is being frozen. Chunky ingredients, like fudge or nuts, are mixed in later. What is the weirdest ice cream flavour you have ever tried?

Ice cream is a tasty treat, but it has lots of fat and sugar in it. It's best not to eat too much ice cream.

Yogurt can be frozen too, but the shop-bought ones still contain lots of sugar. Try making your own with plain yogurt and fresh fruit.

I've got a tangerine lolly!

Ice lollies from the shops have loads of sugar in them. Why not make your own at home using fresh fruit juices?

Nuts and seeds

Nuts and seeds grow on trees and plants. The nuts that we eat, like pecans and almonds, grow inside a hard shell on the tree. We can eat some kinds of seeds too, such as sunflower and pumpkin seeds.

Almonds

Nuts and seeds have fat in them, but it is the sort of fat that is better for our bodies than the fat in snacks like cakes or crisps. It is called unsaturated fat.

Pistachios

Walnuts

Peanuts do not grow on trees. They grow in pods under the ground. That is why they are also called groundnuts.

Nuts and seeds contain protein, vitamins and minerals to help our bodies grow well. They are good for vegetarians who do not get their protein from meat.

Sesame seeds

Watch the salt!

Too much salt is not good for us. Always check that the nuts and seeds you choose have not had lots of salt added to them.

Sunflower seeds

Pumpkin seeds

Crisps and savoury snacks

Next time you go to the supermarket you could try to count all the different sorts of crisps and savoury snacks you see. It might take you a long time!

Crisps are made from thin slices of potato that are fried in big tubs of oil. Then they are put into large, turning drums and sprinkled with different flavourings and salt.

Savoury snacks, like tortilla chips and corn puffs, are made out of maize (or sweetcorn). They come in all sorts of shapes and flavours.

All of these snacks contain fat and lots of salt. If you pack some in your lunchbox try to balance them with a bit of fruit or yogurt and a healthy sandwich.

Raisins

Walnuts

Pistachio nuts

Pumpkin seeds

Almonds

Sunflower seeds and sesame seeds

Have fun with your friends making up your own snack mix. Pop your own popcorn and then mix it with raisins, unsalted nuts and seeds.

My snack mix

Chips

Chips are made out of potatoes. Potatoes are a good energy, or carbohydrate, food but the trouble is that chips are fried in loads of oil. They pack a lot of fat!

Did you know that thin chips are worse for you than fat ones? This is because fat, chunky chips do not soak up quite as much oil as the thin ones.

Eating chips every now and then is all right as long as you are also eating lots of good, healthy stuff, like fruit and vegetables. Having chips every day is loading up your body with lots of fat that can make you unhealthy as you grow up.

What do you like on your jacket potato?

Get your carbohydrates from a jacket potato, rice or pasta instead of chips.

Sweetcorn and tuna is good, but I like cheese and beans too.

23

Pizzas and pies

Pizzas and pies make a tasty snack but they are processed foods. This means that they have had lots of different things done to them to make them ready for us to eat.

Shop-bought pizzas are made in factories.

Freshly made food is much better for us than food that has been through loads of different stages in a factory. It has more vitamins and minerals in it. Processed food often contains too much fat, sugar and salt.

Pizza competition

Make your own pizzas at home with your friends and see who can come up with the most vitamin-packed toppings!

Fast food facts

Fast food is food that is made really quickly and served up fast! Some of it is not very healthy. Look out for fast food that will be better for you. Sandwiches, wraps and salads have good nutrients for your body so try to choose these.

Burgers, hotdogs and chicken nuggets are some favourite fast foods. The meat used in them is not always the best sort. Lots of other things have to be added to it to make it taste all right.

These fast foods are very processed foods. They are full of fat and salt and do not give your body the nutrients it needs.

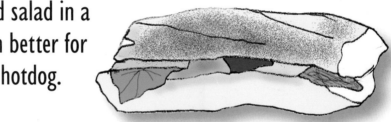

Chicken and salad in a roll is much better for you than a hotdog.

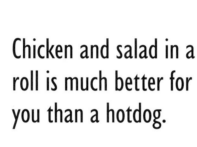

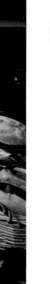

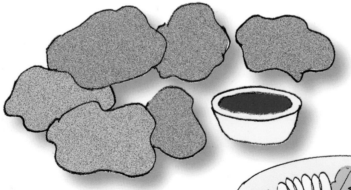

Swap those fatty chicken nuggets for a bowl of pasta salad.

Make your own fast food

If you make your own fast food you will know exactly what ingredients have gone into it. You can also cook it without using lots of extra fat or oil. Always ask an adult to help you when you are cutting things or using the oven.

Wash your hands well before starting to cook.

Pocket a salad

Cut some pitta bread open and stuff it with delicious salad, cheese or cooked chicken.

Nicer nuggets

Cut up some plain chicken breast. Dip it in beaten egg and then breadcrumbs. Bake the nuggets in the oven until golden and crispy.

Add some herbs or spices to the breadcrumbs to make chicken nuggets extra tasty.

Have a healthy day!

Real burgers

Mix up some lean minced meat with some chopped onion. Add chopped herbs, if you like, and a bit of pepper and a little salt. Squish into burger shapes. Then grill the burgers until they are done.

Words to remember

acid   Acids are sour-tasting liquids. Lemon juice and vinegar are acids. Acid in your mouth is made when bacteria eat the sugar in your mouth. This acid then starts to eat into your teeth!

bacteria   Tiny creatures that are so small we cannot see them. Some bacteria are good for us, like the bacteria in yogurt. Some are bad for us and can make us ill.

calcium   A mineral that helps build healthy bones and teeth. Dairy foods, like milk, yogurt and cheese, have calcium in them.

carbohydrates   These are the starches and sugars in food that give us energy. Carbohydrate foods are rice, pasta, bread and potatoes.

fibre   Fibre is found in plant foods like grains and vegetables. It helps our insides to work properly.

flavourings   These are added to foods to change the way they taste. Some flavourings are natural, like herbs and spices. Other flavourings are man-made. Processed foods often contain lots of flavourings.

ingredients   Different foods that are mixed together to make something we can eat.

iron   A mineral in food that we need to keep our blood healthy.

lean   Meat without fat on it.

minerals   Nutrients in food that help our bodies work properly. Calcium and iron are minerals.

nutrients   Parts of food that your body needs for energy, to grow healthily and to repair itself.

processed   Many foods are processed which means they go through some changes before they reach your plate. Some foods are more processed than others. Fast foods and ready-made meals are usually highly processed.

protein   Body-building food that makes our bodies grow well and stay healthy.

salt   Salt has been used for hundreds of years to make food taste nice. But too much salt can make your heart unhealthy when you are older. There is a lot of salt in processed and fast food.

savoury   Savoury is the opposite of sweet.

unsaturated   Unsaturated fat is the sort of fat that is found in vegetable oils, nuts, seeds and oily fish. It is better for you than saturated fat which is found in cakes, biscuits, pies, ice cream, chocolate and many processed foods.

vitamins   Nutrients in food that help our bodies work properly.

Index

WEBSITES

General food information for all ages
www.bbc.co.uk/health/healthy_living/nutrition

Food Standards Agency – healthy eating,
food labelling
www.eatwell.gov.uk

Quizzes and games on food
www.coolfoodplanet.org

Information and games on healthy eating
www.lifebytes.gov.uk/eating/eat_menu.html

Worksheets and activities
www.foodforum.org.uk

Practical advice on healthy eating
www.fitness.org.uk